THE LITTLE BOOK
OF HOLY GRATITUDE

the LITTLE BOOK of
HOLY
GRATITUDE

Compiled from the works of
FR. FREDERICK WILLIAM FABER

SOPHIA INSTITUTE PRESS
Manchester, New Hampshire

Sophia Institute Press
Box 5284, Manchester, NH 03108
1-800-888-9344

www.SophiaInstitute.com

Sophia Institute Press® is a registered trademark of Sophia Institute.

Library of Congress Cataloging-in-Publication Data

Names: Faber, Frederick William, 1814-1863, author.
Title: The little book of holy gratitude / compiled from the works of Fr.
   Frederick William Faber.
Description: Manchester, New Hampshire : Sophia Institute Press, 2016. |
   Originally published under title: On thanksgiving : London : R. and T.
   Washbourne, 1911. | Includes bibliographical references.
Identifiers: LCCN 2016015532 | ISBN 9781622823437 (pbk. : alk. paper)
Subjects: LCSH: Gratitude—Religious aspects—Christianity.
Classification: LCC BV4647.G8 F33 2016 | DDC 241/.4—dc23 LC record
available at https://lccn.loc.gov/2016015532

First printing

CONTENTS

NOTE

The following pages from Fr. Faber are, for the most part, from the seventh chapter of his most popular work, *All for Jesus*. The incidental words at its beginning have been omitted; but a page from *The Creator and the Creature*, showing how radical gratitude is in religion, has been prefixed to it, and a few pages on that virtue have been added from *The Blessed Sacrament*. Where possible we have provided the dates of persons mentioned by Fr. Faber and the names of the creators of the images.

THE LITTLE BOOK
OF HOLY GRATITUDE

Thankful Souls Are Happy

The love of gratitude is preeminently a mindful love. It ponders things and lays them up in its heart, as our Blessed Lady did. It meditates fondly on the past, as Jacob did.

It sings of old mercies and makes much of them, like David in the psalms. Whereas another has the memory of his sins continually before him, a soul possessed with the love of gratitude is perpetually haunted by a remembrance of past benefits; and his abiding sorrow for sin is a sort of affectionate and self-reproachful reaction from his wonder at the abundant loving-kindness of God.

The hideousness of sin is all the more brought out when the light of God's love is thrown so strongly on it. Hence it comes to pass that a very grateful man is also a deeply penitent man; and as the excess of benefits tends to lower us in our own esteem, so we are humble in proportion to our gratitude. But this love does not rest in the luxurious sentiment of gratitude. It breaks out into actual and ardent thanksgiving, and its thankfulness is not confined to words.

Promptitude of obedience, heroic effort, and joyful perseverance: these are all tokens of the love of gratitude.

It is loyal to God.

Loyalty is the distinguishing feature of its service. It is constantly on the lookout for opportunities and makes them when it cannot find them, to testify its allegiance to God; not as if it were doing any great thing, or as if it were laying God under any obligation, but as if it were making payment, part payment and tardy payment, by little installments, for the immensity of His love.

It is an exuberant, active, bright-faced love, very attractive and therefore apostolic, winning souls, preaching God unconsciously, and although certainly busied about many things, yet all of them the things of God.

Happy the man whose life is one long Te Deum! He will save his soul, and not his alone, but many others also. Joy is not a solitary thing, and he will come at last to his Master's feet, bringing many others rejoicing with him, the resplendent trophies of his grateful love.

2

GRATITUDE BRINGS
MANY BLESSINGS

God's mercy is the great feature of the two kingdoms of nature and of grace. Gratitude is man's answer to God's mercy; and just as charity to our neighbor is the best test of our real love of God, so gratitude to our neighbor for his kindness to us is a clearer proof of a grateful disposition than gratitude to God, which is mixed up with so many other cogent considerations.

If we realize everything as coming from God, then these benefits are from Him; and they come from Him in the most beautiful and touching way, through the mediation of our brother's human heart inspired by grace. So every kindness we receive is a little copy of the Incarnation, a miniature of that attractive mystery.

Gratitude increases humility

Gratitude is grounded in humility, and, as usual, increases the grace from which it takes its rise. Heroic humility fancies that wrong is the only right which is due to it. The least kindness seems disproportionately great to a keen and delicate sense of our own unworthiness. The wonder is that anybody should be kind to us at all. If they knew us as we know ourselves, they would have to do holy violence to themselves to show us common courtesy, as great violence as the saints did to themselves when they licked the ulcers of the lepers.

Gratitude increases charity

Again, what warms the heart more to others than the exercise of gratitude? Uncharitableness to a benefactor seems almost an impossibility. Lear's daughters were monsters. Yet think how hard it is to love anyone, any single one, with real charity, without judging, without criticism, without censoriousness, extenuating the evil, believing against appearances, magnifying the good, rejoicing in his virtues.

It is much if each man has one person upon the earth to whom he really feels thus. It is an immense help to his sanctification, a real talent for which he will have account to give.

I doubt its being common, at least in its evangelical purity. Gratitude to benefactors is on the road to it, and not far distant.

Gratitude is contagious

Then again, gratitude is eloquent, graceful, and persuasive as a missionary. It is not only a virtue in ourselves, but it makes others good and virtuous also. It is a blessedly humbling thing to be loved, a veritable abasement to be affectionately respected by those about us.

Gratitude also makes our benefits to others look so little that we long to multiply and enlarge them, while it softens our hearts and unties from them all manner of little antipathies, mean jealousies, petty rivalries, and cold suspicions.

Gratitude nurtures holiness

Lastly, it is the proper and normal state of a holy creature to perfect himself under the continual feeling of obligations that he never can repay. This is the relation between the Creator and himself.

Meanwhile to all the evil and baser parts of our nature it is a real mortification to have the sense of obligation pressing upon us. It is the sign of a vulgar man that he cannot bear to be under an obligation.

Thus, in both ways the sense of obligation is a great part of sanctity. A grateful man cannot be a bad man; and it would be a sad thing indeed, if either in the practice or the esteem of this virtue, the heathen should surpass the disciples of that grateful Master who, to the end of time and in the busy pageant of the judgment, will remember and repay the cup of cold water given in His Name.

3

WE NEGLECT GRATITUDE
MORE THAN PRAYER

If we had to name any one thing that seems unaccountably to have fallen out of most men's practical religion altogether, it would be the duty of thanksgiving. It is not easy to exaggerate the common neglect of this duty. There is little enough of prayer; but there is still less of thanksgiving. For every million Our Fathers and Hail Marys that rise up from the earth to avert evils or to ask graces, how many do you suppose follow after in thanksgiving for the evils averted or the graces given?

Alas! It is not hard to find the reason for this. Our own interests drive us obviously to prayer; but it is love alone that leads to thanksgiving. A man who wants only to avoid hell knows that he must pray; he has no such strong instinct impelling him to thanksgiving.

It is the old story. Never did prayer come more from the heart than the piteous cry of those ten lepers who beheld Jesus entering into a town.[1] Their desire to be heard made them courteous and considerate. They stood afar off, lest He should be angry if they with their foul disease came too near Him.

Alas! They did not truly know that dear Lord or how He had lowered Himself to be counted as a leper for the sons of men. They lifted up their voices, saying, "Jesus, Master, have mercy on us." When the miracle was wrought, the nine went on in selfish joy to show themselves to the priest; but one, only one, and he an outcast Samaritan, when he saw that he was made clean, went back, with a loud voice glorifying God, and he fell on his face before our Savior's feet, giving thanks.

Even the Sacred Heart of Jesus was distressed and, as it were, astonished, and He said, "Were not ten made clean? And where are the nine? There is no one found to return and give glory to God but this stranger!"

How many a time have we not caused the same sad surprise to the Sacred Heart!

[1] See Luke 17:12-19.

When the neglect of a duty is as shocking as is surely the neglect of thanksgiving, it is desirable to show the amount of obligation that rests on us in the matter; and this can best be done by the authority of Scripture.

St. Paul tells the Ephesians that we are to be "giving thanks always for all things, in the name of our Lord Jesus Christ, to God and the Father."[2] Again, we are "to abound unto all simplicity, which worketh through us thanksgiving to God."[3] The Philippians are admonished, "Be nothing solicitous; but in everything by prayer and supplication with thanksgiving let your petitions be made known to God."[4] To the Colossians the apostle Paul says, "As ye have received Jesus Christ the Lord, walk ye in Him, rooted and built up in Him, and confirmed in the faith, as also you have learned, abounding in Him with thanksgiving";[5] and again, "Be instant in prayer, watching in it in thanksgiving."[6]

Creatures are said to be created to be received with thanksgiving by the faithful, and by them that have known

[2] Eph. 5:20.
[3] 2 Cor. 9:11.
[4] Phil. 4:6.
[5] Col. 2:6-7.
[6] Col. 4:2.

the truth: "for every creature of God is good, and nothing to be rejected, that is received with thanksgiving."[7] It was the very characteristic of the heathen, that "when they knew God, they have not glorified him as God, nor given thanks."[8]

What is our life on earth but a preparation for our real life in heaven? And yet praise and thanksgiving are the very occupations of our life in heaven. What is the language of the angels, ancients, and living creatures of the Apocalypse, but, "Amen! Benediction and glory, and wisdom, and thanksgiving, honor, and power, and strength, to our God for ever and ever, Amen"?[9]

We are constantly invoking our Blessed Lady, the angels, and the saints, and we know and are sure that they are always praying for us in heaven; yet am I not right in saying that when we make pictures of heaven in our own minds, it is not so often prayer we picture, as praise and thanksgiving?

Nay, sometimes when death has been at hand and the life of heaven has cast its light forward over God's

[7] 1 Tim. 4:4.
[8] Rom. 1:21.
[9] Apoc. 7:12 (RSV = Rev. 7:12).

servants, they have seemed almost to forget prayer, and as if they were already in hearing of the angelic songs and had caught the note, they occupy with thanksgiving those awful hours that most of all in life seem to need tremulous petition and the strife of prayer.

Thus, when Blessed Paul of the Cross[10] lay dangerously ill, he passed his days in the utterance of thanksgiving and praise, often repeating with particular devotion those words from the Gloria "We give thanks to Thee for Thy great glory!" This had always been his favorite spontaneous prayer, and he had frequently exhorted his religious to use it whenever they had any particular undertaking in hand, saying with particular earnestness, "For the great glory of God." At other times, prostrating himself in spirit before the throne of the Most Blessed Trinity, he fervently exclaimed, "*Sanctus, sanctus,*"[11] or "*Benedictio et claritas,*"[12] which he used to call the song of paradise.

Now, the Church on earth reflects the Church in heaven; the worship of the one is the echo of the worship

[10] St. Paul of the Cross (1694-1775). He was canonized in 1867, after Father Faber wrote this book.

[11] Holy, holy.

[12] Blessing and glory.

of the other. If the life in heaven is one of praise and thanksgiving, so in its measure must be the life on earth.

The very center of all our worship is the Eucharist; that is, as the word imports, a sacrifice of thanksgiving. Everything catches its tone from this. Everything in the Church radiates out from the Blessed Sacrament. The Spirit of the Eucharist must be found everywhere. Even the Jews felt that all prayer must one day cease, except the prayer of thanksgiving, as Wetstein tells us out of the Talmud.

But we have to do with it now as part of our service of love. Let us suppose that the true idea of worship was the one implied in the common practice of most men that it was simply a matter of prayer to a superior Being.

What relation does this put us in with God?

He is our king, our superior, a keeper of treasures, Himself infinite wealth. We go to Him to ask for something. He is to us what a rich man is to a beggar. Our own interest is the prominent part of the matter.

Or we are afraid of His justice. We desire to be let off our punishment and have our sins forgiven. He is full of pity and will hear us if we are importunate. Taking prayer only as the whole of worship, we can rise no higher than this.

It is all very true and very necessary besides. Prayer can teach us to depend on God, and answered prayer to trust in Him. But Infinite Goodness will not let us rest on such terms with Him. We are to be with Him for all eternity; He is to be our everlasting joy; to know Him and to love Him is life; and the love of Him is the joyful praise of Him forever.

As the spirit of oblation, the permission to give God gifts, at once brings us into a dearer and more familiar relation with God, so also does the spirit of thanksgiving. To thank a benefactor simply to get more from him is not thanksgiving but a flattering form of petition.

We thank God because we love Him, because His love of us touches us, surprises us, melts us, wins us. Indeed, so much is thanksgiving a matter of love that we shall thank Him most of all in heaven, when He has given us His crowning gift of the Beatific Vision, when He has given us all of Himself that we can contain, and so there is nothing left for us to receive.

Thanksgiving is therefore of the very essence of Catholic worship; and as the practice of it increases our love, so does the neglect of it betoken how little love we have.

Ah! If we have reason to pity God, if we may dare so to speak with St. Alphonso,[13] because men sin against His

[13] Probably St. Alphonsus de Liguori (1696-1787).

loving Majesty, still more reason have we to do so when we see how scanty and how cold are the thanksgivings offered up to Him.

Nothing is so odious among men as ingratitude; yet it is the daily and hourly portion of Almighty God. There is no telling what He has done for men; there is no exhausting the mines of His abundant mercy, implied by each one of His titles, Creator, King, Redeemer, Father, Shepherd.

He loves to be thanked, because all He wants of us is love; and that He should be pleased to want it is itself an infinite act of love. He has chosen to put His glory upon our gratitude; and yet we will not give it Him!

What is worst of all, this affront does not come, like open sin, from those who are His enemies, and in whose conversion His compassion can gain such glory among men; but it comes from His own people, from those who frequent the sacraments, and make a profession of piety, from those whom He is daily loading with the special and intimate gifts of His Holy Spirit.

Many of us are shocked at sin and sacrilege; we go sad and downcast in the days of the world's carnival; scandal hurts us; heresy is positive suffering, a pungent bitterness, like smoke in our eyes.

It is well. Yet we too go on refusing God His glory by our neglect of thanksgiving. We could glorify Him so cheaply: and yet it hardly comes into our thoughts.

Can we then be said to love Him truly and really? What have we to do? How often shall I say it? To love God and to give Him glory. God forbid we should so much as dream that we had anything else to do.

Let us, then, go about the world seeking these neglected pearls of our heavenly Father's glory and offering them to Him. How is it that we have the heart to wish to do anything but this? Some of His servants have even desired not to die, that they might stay on earth to glorify Him by more suffering.

Such wishes are not for us; but they may do us good; for they help to show us how little love we have, and I must think that to find this out is everything. I can believe that men are deceived, and think they love God when they do not love Him, or that they wish to love Him and do not know how. But can anyone know how little he loves God, and how easily he can love Him more, and yet not wish to do so? Jesus died to prevent the possibility of this; and can He have died in vain?

You must bear with me if I repeat this once more. We do not find fault with sinners who are living out of the grace of God and away from the sacraments, because they do not make thanksgiving. They have something else to do. They have to do penance, and to reconcile themselves with God, and wash their souls afresh in the Precious Blood of Jesus.

The neglect of thanksgiving is an ingratitude that our dear Lord has to impute to His own forgiven children, who are living in His peace, and in the enjoyment of all His privileges.

Now, this deserves to be especially noted. I do not know if you will agree with me, but to my mind the faults of good people — I do not mean slips and infirmities, but cold, heartless faults — have something especially odious about them. A sin is not so shocking a thing to look at, for all its intrinsic deadliness; and this may be the reason why, in the Apocalypse, God breaks out with such unusual and vivid language about lukewarmness and tepidity.[14]

When the angels asked our Lord as He ascended, "What are those wounds in Thy hands?" how much is insinuated in His reply, "The wounds wherewith I was wounded in the house of my friends!" It would be worthwhile writing a treatise entitled *On the Sins of Good People*; for they are many and various and have a peculiar malice

---

[14] Apoc. 3:16 (RSV = Rev. 3:16).

and hatefulness of their own. Unthankfulness is one of the chief of them.

At least, then, bear this in mind while we are talking of thanksgiving. Here is a matter that has to do entirely with good Catholics, with men and women who pray and frequent the sacraments and form the devout portion of our congregations. If there be any reproach in the matter, it all lies on them.

Really, it is almost a comfort to be able to say this. Dry people are ordinarily so self-righteous that it is a positive comfort to get them up into a corner and to be able to say to them, "Now we have nothing to do with sinners at present; you cannot put the sharp things upon them. You are the guilty people; the reproof is all for you; here is something that, if you do not do and do well for God, you are a wretch. *Wretch*, you know, is the very word, the acknowledged epithet for the ungrateful. Well! And with all your prayers and sacraments, you do not do it. It is an ugly inference you will have to draw. Yet why not take a good heart, both you and I, and say an honest Confiteor and arrange with God for a little more grace, and then He shall see how different our future practice is to be?"

From the particular faults of good people, deliver us, O Lord!

There are sacraments for sin; for lukewarmness there are none; nay, worse than none; for who does not know that has ever ministered to souls, how even frequent Communion hardens tepid hearts? Have you ever known ten persons plunged in lukewarmness who were cured? And what was it that cured nine out of the ten? The shame that followed falls into downright sin! Alas! This is a desperate game to play, to expect the prisons of hell to do the work of the medicines of heaven, and stake eternity on the experiment!

The Bible is a revelation of love, but it is not the only one. There is to each one of us a special and personal revelation of divine love in the retrospect of that fatherly providence that has watched over us through our lives.

Who can look back on the long chain of graces of which his life has been composed since the hour of his baptism without a feeling of surprise at the unweariedness and minuteness of God's love? The way in which things have been arranged for his happiness or his welfare, obstacles disappearing as he drew nigh to them, and, just when they looked most insurmountable, temptations turning to his good, and what seemed chastisements as he faced them, changing to love when he looked back upon them.

Every sorrow has found its place in his life, and he would have been a loser if he had been without it. Chance acquaintances have had their meaning and done their work; and somehow it seems as if foreseeing love itself could not have woven his web of life differently from what it is, even if it had woven it of love alone.

He did not feel it at the time. He did not know God was so much with him; for what more unostentatious than a father's love?

When Jacob made his pillow of the cold stones and lay down to sleep, where he had his vision of the ladder, he saw nothing uncommon in the place; but when he awoke out of sleep, he said, "Indeed, the Lord is in this place, and I knew it not."[15]

When Moses desired to see God, the Lord set him in a hole of the rock, and protected him with His right hand while His intolerable glory was passing by, and He said, "I will take away my hand, and thou shalt see my back; but my face thou canst not see."[16]

This is ever God's way. With us He is tender, loving, considerate, forgiving. Our hearts burn within us, as did

[15] Gen. 28:16.
[16] Cf. Exod. 33:23.

the hearts of the two disciples as they walked and talked with Jesus on the road to Emmaus; but it is not until He vanishes from our sight that we know of a truth that it was our dear Lord Himself.[17]

Thus it is that we can come to know God only by meditation. We must ponder things as Mary did. We must muse and be pensive as Isaac was. We must treasure up God's mercies, and make much of them, and set store by them, as did Jacob and David. Jacob was always looking back on his adventurous life; God was to him the God of Bethel, the God of Abraham, the Fear of Isaac. What was David's reproach to his people, but that they forgot God who had done great things in Egypt, wondrous works in the land of Ham, and terrible things in the Red Sea?[18]

The blessings that we know of are more than enough to kindle the most fervent love. Yet we shall never know the half until the Day of Judgment.

Who are we that God should have been thus legislating for us, and laying Himself out to please us? Has He had no world to govern? Has He had no creatures but our own poor selves, or none wiser, holier, and lovelier?

[17] See Luke 24:13-32.
[18] Cf. Ps. 105:21-22.

Yet we tease ourselves about predestination and eternal punishment. We reason harshly about what we cannot alter, and do not understand. I must think this is most unreasonable. For look how the case stands. We know an immense deal about God, yet little or nothing beyond what He has been pleased to reveal to us. Hence, when we argue against Him, our arguments are in reality founded not so much on what we see as on what He has been so good as to tell us about Himself.

Now, here we ought to observe—and people for the most part do not observe it—that God has chiefly illuminated for us His mercy and condescension. His severity is not only the dark side of His most dread majesty, because of its fearfulness, but also because He has told us so little about it.

When love is in question, He has been copious, explicit, minute. He explains, He repeats, He gives reasons, He argues, He persuades, He complains, He invites, He allures, He magnifies.

Of His rigor He drops but a word now and then. He puts it out as a fact and leaves it. He startles by an abrupt disclosure, but, as He startles only out of love, He is at no pains to explain, to soften, to harmonize.

Nay, the most startling expressions about His judgments are rather outbursts from His astonished creatures,

Job, Isaiah, Peter, or Paul, than revelations from Himself. This very fact is itself a fresh instance of His love. Can we not take the hint that His merciful wisdom vouchsafes to give us by this method of proceeding?

As we see but one side of the moon, so we see but one side of God: and what can we know of what we do not see?

There is no end to the variety of the disclosures of His goodness, the inventions of His compassion, and the strangeness of His yearning over His creatures. He has striven to fix our gaze upon these, but we will not have it so. We are busiest with what He wishes us to think least of; and we neglect to ponder all those numberless signs of our heavenly Father's love, which are personal things between Him and ourselves, positive and sensible touches of His unutterable affection!

While God is turning everything to love, and contriving everything for love, how perversely are we trying to thwart His tenderness and long-suffering!

Consider what it is to be blessed by God. Put yourself into the scales, and weigh yourself against Him; and then see what it is to be thought of by Him, to occupy His attention, to try His patience, to call out His love!

Truly, the very thought of God is a bed on which we can lie down and rest whenever we choose. The remembrance of His uncontrolled sovereignty is a joy to us greater than the vision of an angel, brighter than Mary's face, even when it shall smile its "welcome to heaven" on our purified and forgiven souls.

That He is such a God as He is, is more, far more than rest: it is joy and bliss. That He has loved us with an eternal love, and is our own dearest Father, is joy that has no name. It is heaven begun already upon earth!

Is it not, then, one of the wonders of the world that there should be so little thanksgiving, a greater wonder even than that there should be so little prayer, and almost as great a wonder as that God should love us so unutterably?

4

THE SAINTS EVER
GAVE THANKS TO GOD

Thanksgiving has been in all ages the characteristic of the saints. Thanksgiving has been their favorite prayer; and when their love has been grieved because men were unthankful, they have called on the animals, and even on inanimate creatures, to bless God for His goodness.

St. Lawrence Justinian[19] has a beautiful passage on thanksgiving in chapter 28 of his *Treatise on Obedience*:

> Whosoever should try to lay open all God's blessings to the full would be like a man trying to confine in a little vase the mighty currents of the wide ocean;

---

[19] St. Lawrence Justinian (1381-1456).

for that would be an easier work than to publish
with human eloquence the innumerable gifts of God.
Yet although these are unspeakable, both from their
multitude, their magnitude, and their incomprehen-
sibility, they are by no means to be concealed in
silence, or left without commemoration, although
it be impossible to commemorate them adequately.
They are to be confessed with the mouth, revered in
the heart, and religiously worshipped, as far as the
littleness of man can do so. For although we cannot
explain them in words, we can make acknowledg-
ment of them in the pious and enlarged affection
of our hearts. Indeed, the immense mercy of our
Eternal Creator condescends to approve not only
what man can do, but what he would desire to do;
for the merits of the just are counted up by the Most
High, not only in the doing of the work, but in the
desire of the will.

In one of the revelations of St. Catherine of Siena,[20]
God the Father tells her that thanksgiving makes the
soul incessantly delight in Him, that it frees men from

[20] St. Catherine of Siena (1347-1380).

28

negligence and lukewarmness altogether and makes them anxious to please Him more and more in all things.

Our Lord gives the increase of thanksgiving as a reason to St. Bridget[21] for the sacrifice of the Mass. "My body," says He, "is daily immolated on the altar, that men may love me so much the more, and more frequently call to mind my blessings."

"Happy is he," says St. Bernard,[22] "who, at every grace he receives, returns in thought to Him in whom is the fullness of all graces; for if we show ourselves not ungrateful for what He has given us, we make room for still further graces in ourselves." In another place he says, "Speak to God in thanksgiving, and you will get graces more and more abundantly."

So St. Lawrence Justinian says, "Only let God see you are thankful for what He has given you, and He will bestow more gifts upon you, and better gifts."

St. Mary Magdalene of Pazzi[23] also received a revelation, in which she was told that thanksgiving prepared the soul for the boundless liberality of the Eternal Word.

[21] St. Bridget of Sweden (1303-1373).
[22] St. Bernard of Clairvaux (1090-1153).
[23] St. Mary Magdalene of Pazzi (1566-1607).

Now stop, dear reader, and meditate for a few minutes on the Eternal Word: remember which of the three Divine Persons He is, the Second Person, the eternally begotten Word of the Father, the splendor of His Majesty, uncreated Wisdom, the same Person who was incarnate and crucified for us, the same who sent us the Holy Spirit, who gave us Mary, who gives us Himself in the Blessed Sacrament, in whose mind revolves at this moment the countless lusters of all possible creations; then think what His liberalities must be — no bound or measure to them. We cannot count their number, nor exhaust their freshness, nor understand their excellence, nor hold their fullness, nor give intelligible human names to their kinds, inventions, varieties, and wonders.

Oh, that we had greater devotion to the Person of the Eternal Word, that we would read about Him the wonders the Church can tell us, and then meditate and make acts of love on what we read! This is the true way to increase our devotion to His most dear humanity, and to learn how to watch at His Crib, to weep over His Cross, to worship at His tabernacle, and to nestle in His Sacred Heart.

Ask St. Michael, St. John the Evangelist, and St. Athanasius,[24] to get you this devotion; they have a specialty

[24] St. Athanasius (c. 296-373).

for it; and see how you will run the way of God, when its heat has made a furnace of your heart.

Remember also that He Himself has told us, through this revelation to His servant, that thanksgiving prepares the soul for His amazing liberalities.

You see, you must begin this day and hour quite a new and more royal sort of thanksgiving than those mere infrequent, formal, respectful civilities by which you have heretofore been content to acknowledge your accumulated obligations to our dearest Lord. Now promise Him this, and then, with a hotter heart, read on.

St. Bonaventure,[25] or rather the author of the meditations on the life of Christ, tells us that our Blessed Lady gave thanks to God without intermission, and lest in common greetings she should be distracted from the praises of God, she used to reply, when anyone saluted her, "Thanks be to God!" and from her example several saints have adopted the same practice.

The Jesuit Father Didacus Martinez, called the Apostle of Peru because of his zeal for souls and his indefatigable labors in that province, used to say daily four hundred times, and often six hundred times, "Deo gratias," and

[25] St. Bonaventure (1221-1274).

he had some beads on purpose to be accurate. He tried to induce others to practice the same devotion, and he declared that he knew there was no short prayer more acceptable to God, if only it be uttered with a devout intention. It is also mentioned of him in the summary of his process for canonization that his distinct acts of divine love often amounted to several thousands in the day.

Lancisius[26] quotes from Philo[27] a beautiful tradition among the Jews, to this effect: when God had created the world, He asked the angels what they thought of this work of His hands. One of them replied that it was so vast and so perfect that only one thing was wanting to it, namely, that there should be created a clear, mighty, and harmonious voice that should fill all the quarters of the world incessantly with its sweet sound, thus day and night to offer thanksgiving to its Maker for His incomparable blessings.

Ah! They knew not how much more than that the Blessed Sacrament was one day to be! Thus, our thanksgiving should not be an exercise of devotion practiced now and then. It should be incessant, the voice of a love that is ever living and fresh in our hearts.

[26] Nicholas Lancisius, S.J. (1574-1652).
[27] Philo of Alexandria (25 B.C-A.D.50).

In several of the texts that I have already quoted, St. Paul speaks of prayer with thanksgiving: as if there was to be no prayer of which thanksgiving did not form a part; and this also would illustrate what I said of the spirit of the Eucharist being found in every part and act of Catholic devotion.

"I think," says St. Gregory of Nyssa,[28]

that if our whole life long we conversed with God without distraction, and did nothing but give thanks, we should really be just as far from adequately thanking our heavenly Benefactor as if we had never thought of thanking Him at all. For time has three parts — the past, the present, and the future. If you look at the present, it is by God that you are now living; if the future, He is the hope of everything you expect; if the past, you would never have been if He had not created you. That you were born was His blessing; and after you were born, your life and your death were, as the apostle Paul says, equally His blessing.[29] Whatever your future hopes may be, they hang also upon His blessing. You are master

[28] St. Gregory of Nyssa (ca. 335-ca. 395)
[29] Cf. Rom. 14:8.

33

only of the present, and therefore, if you never once intermitted thanksgiving during your whole life, you would hardly do enough for the grace that is always present; and your imagination cannot conceive of any method possible, by which you could do anything for the time past, or for the time to come.

In addition to these authorities, we must not forget to add the number of thanksgivings that have been indulgenced by the Church, in order that she may the more effectually lead her children to glorify God in this way. We shall have occasion, afterward, to revert to the fact that many of these devotions are thanksgivings to the Most Holy Trinity for the gifts and graces bestowed upon our Blessed Lady.

It will be a great practical help to us in thanksgiving to classify the principal blessings for which we are bound continually to thank God; and I propose that we should in this, as in so many other matters, follow the order and method proposed by Father Lancisius.

5

What We Should
Give Thanks For

First of all, we should thank God for the blessings that are common to the whole human race. St. John Chrysostom[30] is very strong upon this point; and our Lord called the practice of thanksgiving for these blessings the necklace of His spouse; for, after He had been pleased to espouse St. Bridget, and was instructing her how she should spiritually adorn herself, He said:

> The spouse ought to have the signs of the Bridegroom upon her breast; that is, the memory of the favors I have shown thee — namely, how nobly I have created thee, giving thee both a body and a

---

[30] St. John Chrysostom (ca. 349-407).

soul; how nobly I have endowed thee with health and temporal blessings; how sweetly I have brought thee back from thy wanderings, by dying for thee, and, if thou wilt have it, restoring to thee thine inheritance.

Orlandini[31] mentions this as one of the characteristics of Father Peter Faber.[32] He was always gratefully mindful not only of God's private blessings but of those common to all mankind. He never forgot that thanks were due to the divine liberality, not less for these common blessings than for special ones; and it was a source of grief to him that men generally paid no attention to them, but took them as matters of course.

He mourned because men rarely blessed that sweet will and boundless charity of God, by which He had first created the world, and then redeemed it, and after that prepared for us eternal glory, and that in all this He had vouchsafed to think specially and distinctly of each one of us.

Under this head of common blessings must be reckoned all the graces of the sacred humanity of Jesus, the

[31] Niccolo Orlandini, S.J. (1554-1606) wrote a history of the Jesuit Order.
[32] Peter Faber, S.J. (1506-1546).

glorious privileges of the Mother of God, and all the splendor of the angels and the saints.

Among other promises that God made to St. Gertrude,[33] this was one: "Whenever anyone devoutly praises God, and gives Him thanks for the blessings conferred upon Gertrude, the Almighty mercifully wills to enrich him with as many spiritual graces as he offers thanksgivings, if not at the present time, at least on some fitting occasion."

In like manner Orlandini tells us that Peter Faber continually used to congratulate the angels and the blessed on their gifts, assiduously pondering the particular graces God had given them; and then separately, for each of them, naming those he could, with great emotion he gave God thanks for them on their behalf.

He reckoned that this was in the highest degree delightful to those inhabitants of heaven, as well as immeasurably profitable to ourselves, as in heaven the blessed see how the debt of gratitude they owe to God is simply oppressive and never can be paid. He practiced this devotion, until at last he came to feel as if there was not a single token of the divine goodness shown to anyone, for which he was not personally a debtor.

[33] St. Gertrude (1256-1302).

He made himself a kind of vicar for everyone who had any sort of happiness or success; and no sooner did he perceive it than he set to work to bless God and to give thanks. There was nothing joyous, nothing prosperous, that he saw or heard of and did not at once became its voice of praise and thanksgiving to the Lord.

Fair cities, fruitful fields, beautiful olive grounds, delightful vineyards—he looked around on them with exulting eye, and because they could not speak for themselves, he spoke for them and thanked the Lord of all for their beauty and, in the name of their owners and possessors, for the dominion thereof that He had given them.

How wonderful must have been the interior of this holy Father's soul, decked with such various and surpassing gifts, enriched with such very particular and, so to speak, private graces, and above all, with a dower of *interior dispositions*, which was his special characteristic treasure and wherein hardly any canonized saint seems to surpass him.

No wonder St. Francis Xavier[34] added him to the litany of the saints, or that St. Francis de Sales[35] speaks of his joy

[34] St. Francis Xavier (1506-1552)
[35] St. Francis de Sales (1567-1622)

and consolation at consecrating an altar in the good Father's native village in Savoy. Yet, like Balthazar Alvarez,[36] whom St. Teresa[37] saw in vision higher in glory than all his contemporaries, although there were many canonized among them, so Peter Faber is not raised upon the altars of the Church, but rests in God's bosom as one of His hidden saints.[38]

Blessed be the Most Holy Trinity for every gift and grace that ever beautified his soul and for all the treasures of grace that God has given to His saints and now keeps hidden in Himself, so that we cannot glorify Him for them!

For personal blessings received

The second class of the divine mercies, for which we are bound to offer continual thanksgiving is obviously the multitude of personal blessings that we ourselves have received from the unmerited goodness of God.

---

[36] Balthazar Alvarez, S.J. (1533-1580) was St. Teresa of Ávila's spiritual director for a time.

[37] St. Teresa of Ávila (1515-1582).

[38] Peter Faber was canonized in 2013 by Pope Francis.

How beautifully St. Bernard expresses this in his first sermon on the Canticles:

> In the wars and conflicts that at no hour are wanting to those who live devoutly in Christ, whether from the flesh, the world, or the devil, for man's life is a warfare on the earth, as you have all experienced in yourselves — in all these conflicts we must daily renew our songs of gratitude for the victories already obtained. As often as a temptation is overcome, or a vice subdued, or an imminent danger avoided, or a snare of the evil one discovered in time, or an old inveterate passion of the soul healed, or a virtue long coveted and prayed for, at length by the gift of God granted to us, what must we do, but, according to the prophet, utter the voice of praise and thanksgiving, and bless God at each single blessing for all His gifts? Else, when the last day comes, he will be reckoned among the ungrateful, who cannot say, "Thy justifications were the subject of my song in the place of my pilgrimage." Nay, at every advance we make, according to the ascensions that each has disposed in his heart, so many separate songs must we sing to the praise and glory of Him who has thus promoted us.

Father Lancisius says:

I would urge all who serve God fervently and faithfully to return Him thanks with particular affection and zealous gratitude, at least four times in the day, for all the personal blessings He has been pleased to confer upon us: first, in the morning, at meditation; secondly, in the middle of the day, or before dinner; thirdly, in the examen of conscience; and fourthly, at bedtime.

The first rank among these personal blessings should be held by the grace that has called us either from heresy to the Catholic Faith, or from neglecting the sacraments to a good life, or from relapses into sin to a real conversion.

Our Lord said once to St. Bridget, "The Bride should be ready, with fair and clean adornments, when the Bridegroom comes to the nuptials, and then are your ornaments clean when you think with gratitude about your sins, how I cleansed you in baptism from the sin of Adam, and how, when you fell, I have so often borne with you, and when else you would have fallen, have held you up."

Among our personal blessings we must thank God for the continuance of health and life, whereby we can daily amass huge treasures of merits and glorify the dear majesty of God by numerous acts of love.

We must thank Him also for past and present humiliations, for calumnies, unkind interpretations of our words, unloving deeds, inconsiderate omissions, or unfriendly intentions, the detractions we have suffered from, and everything that has ever happened to mortify our self-love. For, if we consider the true interests of our soul, it is a real blessing to be humbled and kept down, not only because it helps us to advance in the way of perfection, but also because of the innumerable opportunities it gives us of glorifying God and acquiring merit, and of being so much higher in heaven. Indeed, there is hardly anything by which we can glorify God more effectually than by the exercise of virtues while we are under humiliations.

So, if we are in a condition or state of life in which we do not attract the notice or the praise of men, we ought to thank God most warmly for it, considering the danger there would be to our souls in a more elevated and honorable state.

The patience and long-suffering of God should be another subject of continual thanksgiving. Is it not wonderful how He has borne with us, and we so miserably perverse the while?

How many absolutions have we not had, our lost merits restored to us, fresh graces given us! What a miracle of patience God has been! Can we not well enter into the spirit of that Spanish lady of whom Father Rho speaks, who said that "if she had to build a church in honor of the attributes of God, she would dedicate it to the Divine Patience"? How beautiful her soul must have been, and how many deep and intimate things must have passed between her and God!

Again, how many sins have we been in the way of committing, or near to committing, and by grace have not done so! How many temptations have proved fatal to others, which never so much as came in our way! Even the heathen emperor Antoninus[39] thanked God for the occasions of sin to which he had never been exposed. This, then, is another personal blessing for which we must always give thanks.

Again, there are three blessings that a Catholic ought to remember at every time: the divine election that made him a Catholic, and not a Jew, Mahometan, or heretic; the divine providence that has been his shield and buckler ever since he was born; and the divine liberality that has

[39] Antoninus (85-161), Roman emperor.

loaded him with such a profusion of gifts and graces, not absolutely necessary for his salvation, but either to adorn his soul or to increase his joy in Christ.

St. Chrysostom would also have us remember with special gratitude the hidden and unknown blessings that God has heaped upon us. "God," he says, "is an over-running fountain of clemency, flowing upon us, and round about us, even when we know it not."

Orlandini tells us that in this matter Father Peter Faber was remarkable. He used to say there were hardly any blessings we ought more scrupulously to thank God for than those we never asked and those that come to us without our knowing it. It is not unlikely, in the case of many of us, that these hidden blessings may turn out on the last day to have been the very hinges on which our lives turned and that through them our predestination has been worked out and our eternal rest secured.

For afflictions and tribulations

Neither must we think that too much is being asked of us when spiritual writers tell us we ought to return thanks to God for afflictions and tribulations, both those that are passed and those that we may be suffering from at the present time. This is, of course, not the place to enter into the uses and merciful purposes of affliction. But they will readily suggest themselves to everyone. St. John of Ávila[40] used to say that one Deo gratias in adversity was worth six thousand in prosperity.

But we must again refer to Orlandini in his description of the special gift of thanksgiving that Peter Faber possessed. He thought it was not enough that men should humble themselves under the hand of God in the time of public calamities, but that they should give God hearty thanks for them, for famine and scarcity, for wars, floods, pestilences, and all the other scourges of heaven: and it was a subject of vehement sorrow to him that men did not openly acknowledge God's merciful intentions in these things.

When he grieved over the misfortunes of others, what stirred his sorrow most was that men did not see how much gentleness there was in the visitation; for it is not perfect gratitude that is fed by favors only. "Nay, we cannot tell," says St. Antiochus, "who is really grateful till we see whether he gives God hearty and sincere thanks in the midst of calamities"; and St. Chrysostom, in his *Homilies on the Epistle to the Ephesians*, says that we ought to thank

[40] St. John of Ávila (1499-1569).

God for hell itself, and for all the pains and punishments that are there, because they are such an effectual bridle to our inordinate passions.

For trifling blessings

It is also a very important devotion to thank God for what we call trifling blessings. Not of course that any goodness of God is trifling to such as we are; but mercies may be little by comparison.

St. Bernard applies to this devotion our Lord's injunction to His disciples to gather up the fragments that nothing be lost. In the *Life of the Blessed Battista Varani*,[41] a Franciscaness, we read that our dear Lord once said to her, "If you were never to sin again, and if you alone were to do more penances than all the blessed in heaven have ever done, and if you were to shed as many tears as would fill all the seas, and suffer as many pains as you are capable of suffering, all that would not be enough to thank me for the very least blessing I have ever bestowed upon you."

Another time Battista said that God had given her to understand that the glorious Mother of God, and all men

[41] Blessed Battista Varani (1458-1524).

and angels with their perfections, could not adequately thank the Divine Love for the creation of the least field flower on the earth, which He had made for our use, in respect of the infinite gulf there is between His excellence and our vileness.

Orlandini tells us that Peter Faber excelled in this devotion also; and that he used to say that in every gift of God, no matter how trifling, three things were to be considered: the giver, the gift, and the affection with which it was given; and that, if we pondered these three points, we should see that there could be no such things as little mercies. Doubtless, this was the reason, says the biographer, why that blessed mind was always overflowing with the abundance of divine gifts.

For, as God is an inexhaustible ocean of goodness, the fountain of His liberality cannot be dried up where He meets with a considerate and thankful mind into which He can pour Himself. Thomas à Kempis observes that if we look at the dignity of the Giver, no gift is small that comes from God.[42]

[42] Thomas à Kempis (1380-1471), *The Imitation of Christ*, bk. 2, chap. 35.

For blessings we obstructed

St. Ignatius[43] used to say that there were very few, perhaps not one person, in the world who thoroughly understood what an impediment we are to God's wish to work great things in our souls; for it is hardly credible what God would do if we would only let Him. Hence holy people have made a special devotion of thanking the Divine Majesty for all the blessings He would in His munificence have conferred upon them, if they themselves had not hindered Him.

Others, again, have been touched with sensible gratitude for blessings for which they were not thankful at the time they received them. Peter Faber used to say Masses, or get them said, in expiation of his own and others' ungrateful inconsiderateness when receiving blessings from God; and whenever he saw a rich or fortunate man, he used to make acts of reparation for his possible forgetfulness of his divine Benefactor.

Others have felt strongly about blessings for which they thanked God at the time, but it now seems to them, not so much as they might have done, or so affectionately. St.

---

[43] St. Ignatius (1491-1556).

Lawrence Justinian tells us that this feeling enters into the thanksgivings of the blessed in heaven. Then there are blessings that we have abused or made light of; and St. Bernard tells us these should certainly be made the subject of special thanksgiving.

Others, again, have exercised devotion in thanking God for blessings that others were preparing for them, or that were growing, or that happened while they themselves were asleep. This at least shows the ingenious love of grateful hearts.

But there is another practice recorded by Orlandini of Peter Faber, which must by no means be omitted. It is well worth the imitation of all of us. It is to give God special thanks for preventing innumerable of our words and deeds from giving scandal, when in themselves they are calculated to do so. What can be a sweeter mercy than this?

For God's nonrational creatures

Another practice of holy men has been to thank God on behalf of the irrational creatures, a devotion most acceptable to Him as the wise Creator of the world; and it has also the further advantage of being a most excellent practice of the presence of God, enabling us everywhere, and at all times, to rise to Him by means of His creatures.

But we must not in this think so much of the dominion or use that God has given us out of His bounty over these creatures, as of the love that He had toward us in creating them, as He Himself said to St. Catherine of Siena, "The soul that has arrived at the state of perfect love, when it receives gifts and graces from me, does not look so much at my gift as at the affection of charity that moved me to confer the gift upon it."

For blessings given to our enemies

We shall also glorify God by thanking Him for all the blessings conferred upon our enemies. This devotion will be the more acceptable to Him because it is a great exercise of brotherly love; for it is impossible to practice it long without all coldness and uncomfortable feeling giving way to gentleness and tenderness, even toward those who have wronged us most, or who show the greatest dislike of us.

But, as my chief aim in this treatise is nothing but to accumulate an abundance of affectionate contrivances to get our dearest Lord a little more glory, as it is on behalf of the wrongs of God, the injured interests of Jesus, that I want to move my readers, there are some other methods of thanksgiving that are very much to my purpose.

Look at the lost souls! There is not one whom God has not loaded with blessings, and pursued with tenderest graces, and striven to win with the divine caresses of His Holy Spirit. But there are no thanks there. Justice has its harvest there, but not love. Hence it is that Da Ponte[44] in the preface to his *Meditations* recommends to us the practice of thanking God for all the blessings of nature and grace that have been bestowed on those who have lost themselves by their own willfulness.

Nay, there have been some so jealous of God's glory, so afraid that some nook of His creation would not thank Him for His goodness, that they have loved to praise Him because even the lost are for His love's sake punished *citra condignum*, "less than they deserve."

How prodigal has God been of His goodness! Could figures tell the number of His gifts to the multitude of the reprobate? Then add the infidels and heretics now on earth, who leave Him without thanksgiving, and bad Catholics living in mortal sin and trampling the sacraments beneath their feet, crucifying our dearest Lord afresh, and putting Him to an open shame!

[44] Venerable Ludovico da Ponte, S.J. (1554-1624).

Blessed be God for every one of the gifts of every one of these! May the Blessed Sacrament praise Him this hour for them all in every tabernacle throughout the world; for sweeter a thousand times is the cry of that mystical life of Jesus than could have been the strong, clear, ubiquitous, and musical voice that the Jewish tradition dreamed angelic love had craved.

For all God's angels and saints

Another practice of thanksgiving is to thank our Blessed Lord, with the utmost fervor and simplicity of joy, for the immense multitude of angels and saints who fill the choirs of heaven, adoring Him as their head and thanking Him as the author of all grace and the giver of all gifts.

For, if we sincerely love Him, it is our chief sorrow that we cannot love Him worthily, and, therefore, it is really a blessing bestowed upon us that He should have been pleased to create creatures who can love Him so much more, so unspeakably more, than we do.

To this some have added thanksgivings for all the worship and adoration He is receiving at this moment throughout the earth, and in purgatory, all the sacrifices that are being offered, all the prayers that are being made in churches, the vows by which fervent men are binding themselves, and all the increases of divine love that are going on in the hearts of those who are in the state of grace.

Others, again, have been drawn to continual thanksgiving to Jesus for the glorious mysteries of His life, as contrasted with the joyful and the sorrowful, thanking Him for them daily, for the glory He Himself had in them, and for the glory they gave His Father, as well as the benefits that we derive from them.

Thus, those who have had a special devotion to our Lord's Resurrection have almost always coupled it with an equally special attraction to thanksgiving, as they have also mysteriously coupled with it a particular drawing to the attribute of sanctity in God.

For the gift of faith

Others have been distinguished by a deep and lifelong feeling of gratitude for the gift of faith, and for all the supernatural wonders of our holy religion. These form two very distinct sources of devotion.

By the latter, to speak of that first, men are led to rejoice in the absolute sovereignty of God and the unlimited supremacy of His most dear Majesty, and in their own vileness and nothingness. They are drawn, like Peter

Consolini,[45] to the views of grace that seem to make least of man's freedom and most of God's election; or if, like Lessius,[46] they take the other view, it is for the same reason, because to such minds that view is more glorious to God than the other.

They think they can never thank God sufficiently that they are so completely and helplessly in His hands. They would not for the world have it otherwise. They can hardly understand those who do not feel as they do. They bless God for His promises, but their habit of mind is to trust rather to His love.

They do not care about merit. What they care about is His glory. "I cannot bear this talking about merit," said St. Francis de Sales, though it does not follow that everybody else has a right to say what he said.

In low spirits it is the thought of God's sovereignty, rather than of His faithfulness, which is the bed of their repose. These are the persons who are always so happy in religion, except when God withdraws for a while this blessed confidence, for their greater sanctification; and

---

[45] Fr. Peter Consolini (1565-1643) was an Oratorian priest and a disciple of St. Philip Neri (1515-1595).

[46] Probably Leonardus Lessius (1554-1623)

even then their language is that of Job, "Though He slay me, yet will I trust in Him."[47]

Persons with this propensity seem to have a special gift of unselfishness and unworldliness. They delight in the spiritual plans and successes of other men, or of religious orders that are rivals of their own. It is a joy to them that all the arrangements about merit, satisfaction, remission, infused habits and indulgences are so thoroughly supernatural.

They have a profound reverence for all the benedictions of the Church, for her sacramentals, forms, and manipulations, and for the rubrics of her ceremonies, which seem to be rather gleams of heaven than the marshalling of earthly pomps. They glory in the principles of the gospel and the vitality of the Church being opposed to all the calculations and maxims of the world. They revel in the strength of weakness, in the exaltation of holy poverty, in the splendor of abasement, in the almightiness of suffering, in the victory of defeat.

These things are to them like the odors of the Spice Islands wafted out to the weary navigator. They are fragrant of heaven, and of God.

[47] Cf. Job 13:15.

It is a peculiar delight to them that men are converted by unaccountable grace rather than by controversy, and that God so often seems to take matters into His own hands, and to work of Himself, without making use of us.

They have no heart-aching difficulties about God and nature, because they do not look upon men as the center of the system, or the reason of creation, or the mark God worked to. They think this would narrow their spiritual views as much as believing the earth to be the center of the solar system, or the solar system the center of the universe, would narrow a man's views of nature.

They look on Jesus as the center of all things, as the reason of creation, as the mark God worked to, as He vouchsafes to speak of Himself as working, who is self-sufficient bliss and rest. The predestination of Jesus, in their view, explains everything, harmonizes everything, controls everything, and is the fountain of everything that lies outside the unity of the Most Holy Trinity; and Mary's predestination is part of His.

They are only here in His train, and they have no consequence or importance except the one dear dignity of being loved by Him. As the little stars go out when the great sun shines, so faith's hard facts, the permission of evil, and the eternity of punishment — these men can scarcely see, because of the blessed and exhilarating splendor of the predestination of Jesus.

The practice of thanksgiving for the gift of faith is one that cannot be too strongly recommended in our time and country. This was the devotion of that most beautiful soul St. Jane Frances de Chantal;[48] and I quote from volume 2 of her *Life* at length with the less scruple, because of all the varieties of the spiritual life, of all the manifestations of the spirit of holiness, none seems so fitted to ourselves as the sweet and gentle spirit of the Visitation. We read of her as follows:

> When, after her marriage, she went to reside in the country, and again on becoming a widow, she ordered those of her servants who had the best voices to learn the chant of the *Credo*, to assist in singing it more solemnly at the parochial Mass, in which she took very great pleasure; and afterward, when a religious, she occasionally sang it at recreation. She paid a special devotion to the holy martyrs, because they had shed their blood for the

[48] St. Jane Frances de Chantal (1572-1641).

Faith, and to the saints of the first ages, because they had defended that holy Faith by their writings and their labors, so that it became quite a proverb among her nuns, on the festivals of these great saints of the first centuries, to say: "It is one of our Mother's saints!"

She was not satisfied with hearing these Lives read in the refectory, and speaking of them at recreation; but she had the book occasionally taken to her room, to read it again in private, and in the latter years of her life she purchased the *Lives of the Saints* in two volumes, and marked the lives of those great saints and first followers of the Church, which she read with greatest devotion.

She had an especial devotion to St. Spiridion[49] who had captivated the reason of a subtle philosopher with the Creed. She knew by heart the hymn of St. Thomas,[50] "Adoro Te devote," and often recited it. She taught it to some of the Sisters, and told them that she always repeated the following

[49] Probably St. Spyridon (c. 270-348), bishop of Trimythous in Cyprus.
[50] St. Thomas Aquinas (1225-1274).

verse two or three times: *Credo quidquid dixit Dei Filius* (I believe all the Son of God has spoken).

At the commencement of her widowhood, so thoroughly did she abandon herself to her devotion that she had no greater pleasure than in convincing her understanding with the following words: "I see the juice of the grape, and I believe it to be the Blood of the Lamb of God; I taste bread, and I believe it to be the true Flesh of my Savior."

But when she placed herself under the guidance of St. Francis [de Sales], he taught her to simplify her belief and to recite fervent and short acts of faith, thus showing her that the simplest and the most humble faith is also the most loving and most solid.

She daily repeated at the end of the Gospel of the Mass, the *Credo* and the *Confiteor*; and one day, while exhorting her nuns to do likewise, she exclaimed, "O God! What need have we to humble ourselves, inasmuch as we are not deemed worthy to confess our creed before all the tyrants of the earth!"

It was the same spirit which made St. Philip [Neri] rise up in agitation one night in the Oratory, fearing lest what the preacher of the evening had said should give his hearers a favorable idea of the

Institute, and cry out, "There is no need to boast: we are nothing; no one of the Congregation has shed his blood for the Faith yet."

St. Jane Frances had also certain sentences written on the walls of her cell, which was afterward made the novitiate; and she wrote on the wall beneath the crucifix the following verse from the Canticles: "I sat down under the shadow of my well-beloved, and his fruit was sweet to my palate."[51] A Sister begged her to say why she put the sentence in that place. "In order," she replied, "to be often making bare and simple acts of faith; for the faith, though a light in itself, is a shadow to the human reason; and I wish my reason to sit down in repose under the shadow of the faith that makes one believe that He who was placed on that Cross with so much contempt is the true Son of God."

Another time she said that she had always the intention, when looking at the crucifix, that her mere look should be an act of faith similar to that of the centurion, who, striking his breast, said: "Indeed this man was the Son of God."[52]

[51] Cant. 2:3 (RSV = Song of Sol. 2:3).
[52] Mark 15:39.

St. Jane told a person in confidence that while she was yet in the world, God had given her great lights regarding the purity of faith and showed her that the perfection of our understanding in this life is its captivity and subjection to obscure matters of faith and that the understanding would be enlightened in proportion as it should be humbly submissive to these obscurities; and that she always hated those sermons that attempted to prove by natural reason the mystery of the holy and adorable Trinity, and other articles of our Faith; and that the faithful soul must seek no other reason than that sole sovereign universal reason — namely, that God has revealed these things, as far as was needful, to His Church.

She never cared to hear of miracles in confirmation of the Faith, nor revelations, and occasionally she made them pass them over while they were reading in the refectory the *Lives of the Saints* or sermons on the festivals and mysteries of our Lord and our Lady.

St. Jane resembled in this the great St. Louis of France,[53] who, once when he was called into his private chapel to see some miraculous appearance that had taken place at Mass, refused to go, saying that he thanked God he

[53] St. Louis, king of France (1214-1270).

believed in the Blessed Sacrament and should not believe it more firmly for all the miracles in the world; neither did he wish to see one, lest he should thereby forfeit our Lord's special blessing on those who have not seen and yet have believed.[54] She occasionally said to her nuns, "What have we to do with proofs, miracles, and revelations, unless it be to bless God, who has provided them for some who have need thereof? God has revealed to us all that is necessary through His Church."

When she composed the meditations for the retreats, extracted from the writings of St. Francis de Sales, she wished to have one on the incomparable grace we have of being children of Holy Church. She had it written on a separate sheet of paper and told her nuns that she had not gotten beyond this meditation during the whole of the two first days of her retreat.

She read Holy Scripture by the order of her superiors, but, among all the books of this sacred volume, the Acts of the Apostles was her favorite; and it is impossible to say how often she read and reread it. She related to her community its contents with fresh fervor; and it seemed that each time she spoke of this primitive Church, she

[54] See John 20:29.

told them something that they had never heard before. When she heard that her son had been killed in fighting against the English in the Isle of Rhe, she knelt down with clasped hands, her eyes lifted to heaven, and said: "Allow me, my Lord and my God! Allow me to speak, to give vent to my grief; and what shall I say, O my God, unless it be to thank Thee for the honor Thou hast done me in taking my only son while he was fighting for the Church of Rome?"

She then took up a crucifix, which she kissed, and said: "I receive this blow, my Redeemer, with all submission and beseech Thee to receive this child into the arms of Thy Divine Mercy." After this, she thus addressed the deceased: "O my dear son! how happy art thou in having sealed with thy blood the fidelity that thy ancestors have ever had for the Church of Rome; in this I esteem myself happy and return thanks to God for having been thy mother."

Thanksgiving after Communion

But there is one practice of thanksgiving that must enter into all others and be joined to them: thanksgiving, if it might be so, of tears rather than of words; gratitude for the adorable Sacrifice of the Mass, and the Personal Presence of Jesus with His Church.

It is not only the inestimable blessing of the sacrifice that must call out these incessant thanksgivings; neither is it the unspeakable love and condescension involved in it. But it is the joy that now at least thanks are offered to God that are equal to Himself.

We need no longer sit by the waysides of the world, downcast and weeping, because His Blessed Majesty is not worshipped, praised, and thanked as it ought to be. One Mass is infinite praise, and there are Masses nearly every moment of the day and night on this side of the world and at our antipodes. There is the Blessed Sacrament in crowded or neglected churches all the earth over, and, wheresoever He is, there is infinite praise, unspeakable worship, unfathomable thanksgiving!

Indeed, the especial function of the Holy Mass is Eucharist: the worship of thanksgiving! Nay, even the mere creature by means of the Blessed Sacrament can himself attain to a higher act of worship than he could ever else have dreamed of; for the creature can pay no higher homage to his Creator than by receiving Him in the overwhelming reality of the Blessed Sacrament.

What repose there is in the thought of all this! How many inward complainings can we hush by it! How much unhumble disquietude with our own littleness, our own vile attainments, our own impossibilities of loving God as we feel we ought to love Him!

Blessed Jesus! He is all things to us. Whatever we want, it comes to us in the shape of Him, in the strangest of places and the most unaccountable of ways! Shall we not say, then, that we love God worthily and worship Him abundantly, for Jesus is our love and our worship too?

How happy, with an abounding inexhaustible happiness, this makes us! It is so much sweeter to owe everything to Jesus than to have it of ourselves, even if that were possible! There is no pleasure on this side the grave equal to the feeling of the multiplication and reduplication of our obligations to our dear Lord.

The more we run into His debt, the more joy it is; the more inextricable our obligations are, the more light-hearted is our liberty; the knowledge that to all eternity we shall be just as far off from satisfying His love, just in the same impossibility of paying what we owe, is itself the joy of joys.

Meanwhile, thanks, a thousand times thanks, to Jesus! God gets His praise, His worship, and His thanks, deep, beautiful, infinite as Himself.

Now this, perhaps, will enable us to judge how far we are truly grateful to our Blessed Lord and how far we have really discharged the duty of thanksgiving. Whatever may be thought of particular methods of this devotion, practiced by the saints or suggested by spiritual writers, the whole Church is agreed on the duty and fitness of a special thanksgiving after Holy Communion.

If ever there is a time for thanks too deep for words, it is when the Creator has been pleased to overwhelm His creatures with this stupendous gift of Himself, and when He is actually within us. Hence it is that spiritual writers tell us, for a while at least, not to open a book, but to commune with Jesus in our hearts. We must surely have something to say to Him then, or at least He will say something to us in the deep silence of our hearts, if we will only listen. Yet how stands the case in reality?

If we may take the fervor and regularity with which we make our thanksgiving after Communion as an index of our love of Jesus, nothing can well be more disheartening. To many of us there is hardly a quarter of an hour in our lives more tedious, idle, aimless, and unsatisfactory than what we call our thanksgiving. We have nothing to say. Our hearts do not run over.

We never can receive a greater gift in this world. With each Communion, it grows more wonderful; so much does our lukewarmness and ingratitude make the continuance of His love a stranger marvel. He who is to be our joy for all eternity has come, and we have nothing to say to Him. We tire of His company. It is a relief to us when we may believe that He has gone. We have been civil to Him. We have asked His blessing as our superior. But it has been little more than civility; at the most, it was only respect.

Alas! Alas! It is useless to ask men to adopt various practices of thanksgiving, when our Lord's own visit can hardly force one upon them! It is as if thanksgiving had but one fixed home left on earth, and that its tenure even of that was continually becoming more and more precarious.

It will be something, however, if these bad, lazy, listless thanksgivings bring home to us how very, very little in reality we care for Jesus; and that if we could only have His grace without Him, it would be just the religion to our mind.

Ah! Dearest Lord! And knowing all this, Thou abidest in the tabernacle!

But you will say to me, "It is hard of you to leave us in this way with a few ill-humored words. If our thanksgivings are so bad, perhaps we might try to make them better, if we had any hints given us how to do so."

Well! Let us see what our good books can tell us.

I suppose there are few difficulties more universally felt than that of making a good thanksgiving after Communion. Spiritual writers, as I just now said, tell us we ought not to use books, at least not for some time afterward. They assure us that if grace has any special and critical moments in life, they are passing while Jesus remains in our hearts by His sacramental presence.

The great teacher of thanksgiving after Communion is St. Teresa. The stress she lays upon it, the frequency with which she returns to the subject, the practical counsels she gives about it make it quite one of the salient points of her celestial teaching. She was indeed, as a French writer calls her, a "Mother of the Church"; and the whole matter of thanksgiving after Communion was one of her characteristic lessons.

She seems also—such, at least, has been the experience of one of her most enthusiastic clients—to have a special grace from God to enable others to improve in this respect, which is of such surpassing importance to the whole spiritual life.

Good and regular thanksgivings after Mass would be the completest, speediest, and most successful reform of the clergy, while they would also enable the laity either to communicate more frequently or to profit more by their frequent Communion.

If your thanksgivings are poor and wretched, pray to St. Teresa, and she will get you the grace to set them right. She will get you a grace that you will feel quite sensibly in its work within you. All eternity is too short to praise God adequately for any one of His least compassions to us. It would take many eternities to praise Him rightly for having given to us and to His Church our "Seraphic Mother," St. Teresa.

St. Alphonso and others have left it on record that one Communion rightly made is enough to fit a man for canonization and that the thanksgiving is the time when the soul appropriates to itself the abundance of grace, and drinks deepest of the fountains of light and life.

St. Philip's advice was full of his usual gentle wisdom. He recommends that if we have made our meditation before Mass, we should not cast about for new thoughts after Communion but should take up some train of thought that we had found came with unction to us in our meditation. This will prevent a great deal of time being lost in our thanksgiving, from our being at sea for want of a subject, and from having so many things to say to our Lord that we do not know what to say first.

It is of a piece with our saint's quiet ways in spiritual things. He would have us so familiar with our Lord that any unusual or busy reception of Him would rather bespeak the less perfect activity of Martha than the repose and union of Mary. The same spirit made him wish that the Fathers of his Congregation should not have a fixed hour for Mass but should go at once when the sacristan called them.

Many persons living in the world are not able to make any regular meditation before Communion, and many also practice mental prayer in a different way, spending their time in what is called affective prayer, with their will rather than their understanding, and such are sometimes puzzled to find thoughts that they can resume from their prayer when they have received Communion.

Others, again, particularly those who have a very special devotion to the Blessed Sacrament, and yet cannot boast of a habitual union with God, find St. Philip's recommendation unsuited to them and must think more immediately of the Blessed Sacrament and of the presence of Jesus within them at that moment.

There is also another thing in this form of thanksgiving that deserves to be dwelt upon. It brings out so very much the devotion to the Person of the Eternal Word.

The want of this is the cause of much shallowness and of much dryness in prayer; and especially to it may be traced the absence of the deep spirit of adoration that should distinguish the devotion to the Blessed Sacrament, and also the barrenness of soul that frequent Communion seems sometimes rather to increase than to relieve.

Let priests preach and teach the divinity of Jesus, no matter how uninviting may be the notion of theological sermons, and we shall soon see how hearts will melt and how Bethlehem and Calvary will give out their rich depths of tenderness to the poorest and the simplest of Christ's humble poor.

To how many has meditation become a different thing, when they carried to the Crib or the Cross the light of our dear Lord's divinity along with them! Although they were ordinarily in no high state of prayer, nor in the practice of self-crucifying austerities, their prayer, through the refulgence of this one doctrine, has often ended, as if they were very contemplatives, in the bosom of the Most Holy Trinity.

Many have there been who could not put into words what happened to them; but to whose state of mind, for a little while at least, Dante's words would not have been unsuitable:

Then "Glory to the Father, to the Son,
And to the Holy Spirit," rang aloud
Throughout all Paradise, that with the song
My spirit reeled, so passing sweet the strain.
And what I saw was equal ecstasy:
One universal smile it seemed of all things,
Joy past compare, gladness unutterable,
Imperishable life of peace and love,
Exhaustless riches and unmeasured bliss.[55]

[55] Dante, *Paradiso*, canto 27.

6

Three Gifts of Thanksgiving

By this devotion of thanksgiving we can do three things: promote the glory of God, advance the interests of Jesus, and help in the saving of souls.

Thanksgiving gives God glory

First, as to the promotion of the glory of God: He has chosen to rest His glory in great measure on the praise and thanksgiving of His creatures. Thanksgiving was one of the ends for which He created us.

Neither is there any matter in which He is as defrauded of His glory as in this, and none consequently in which He looks more for reparation from His faithful servants.

No one ever thanks Him with devout intention who does not at once and thereby give Him glory. I said that joy came of thanksgiving; and the spirit of thanksgiving seems not only to accompany the joy that is a special fruit of the Holy Spirit but also to be manifested in all the special devotions that have to do with joy.

Those who have had a special devotion to St. Raphael, the angel of joy, have generally had a more than usual gift of thanksgiving. We see this even in the book of Tobias, without coming to the examples of the saints most devoted to that dear spirit, as St. John of God,[56] the Blessed Benvenuta,[57] St. Giacinta Mariscotti,[58] and others.

"Father! He gave joy," says young Tobias about St. Raphael.[59] When Raphael is about to make himself known, he says to them, "Bless ye the God of heaven; give glory to Him in the sight of all that live, because He hath shown His mercy to you. For it is good to hide the secret of a king: but honorable to reveal and confess the works of God."[60]

Again, "When I was with you I was there by the will of God: bless ye Him and sing praises to him."[61] Again, "It is

[56] St. John of God (1495-1550).
[57] Blessed Benvenuta Bojani (1254-1292).
[58] St. Giacinta Mariscotti (1585-1640).
[59] See Tob. 12:2-3.
[60] Tob. 12:6-7.
[61] Tob. 12:18.

time that I return to him that sent me: but bless ye God, and publish all his wonderful works."[62]

Probably as he parted from them, he let them see a glimpse of his angelic beauty, as they immediately went into an ecstasy of three hours, and what it left behind was the spirit of thanksgiving. "Then they, lying prostrate for three hours upon their face, blessed God; and rising up, they told all his wonderful works. And Tobias the elder, opening his mouth, said, 'Give glory to the Lord, ye children of Israel. See what he hath done for us, and with fear and trembling give ye glory to him, and extol the eternal King of worlds. Bless ye the Lord, all his elect, keep days of joy, and give glory to him. Jerusalem, city of God, ... give glory to the Lord for thy good things.'"[63]

Then, how beautiful was his close, after the angel had left his mantle of joy and thanksgiving on the holy old man! "The rest of his life was in joy; and with great increase of the fear of God, he departed in peace."[64] Indeed the joy lived after him, and there was joy instead of mourning for him; for it is said, "And after he had lived

[62] Tob. 12:20.
[63] Tob. 12:22; 13:1, 3, 6, 10-12.
[64] Tob. 14:4.

ninety-nine years in the fear of the Lord, with joy they buried him"[65] — a joy like that which is so often found in religious houses, when God has called one of the community to Himself and which is sometimes almost a scandal to externs who know not the deep unearthly spirit of the cloister.

Thanksgiving assists Jesus

Secondly, thanksgiving gives us great means of furthering the interests of Jesus. What was there upon earth that He sought more vehemently than His Father's glory?

Although it is said of Him that He knew what was in men and would not trust Himself to them, yet He vouchsafed to appear surprised that only one of the ten lepers returned to give thanks to God.[66]

How full also of mystery is that outburst of thanksgiving on His own part, when He thanked His Father, and confessed before Him, because the Father had hidden His mysteries from the wise and prudent, and had revealed them to babes.[67]

[65] Tob. 14:16.
[66] John 2:24; Luke 17:16-17.
[67] Matt. 11:25.

But there is one way especially that I would venture to suggest as a means of promoting the interests of Jesus, and that in a most loving manner and with little trouble to ourselves. It is by assuming to ourselves a little apostolate to spread the practice of thanksgiving.

There are few of us who do not influence some others, children, or servants, or friends. Let us teach them to make more frequent, more systematic, more fervent thanksgiving. Let us say a seasonable word for this practice whenever we can. If each of us persuaded five people, in honor of our dear Lord's Five Wounds, to make daily thanksgiving, these five would in turn spread it to others, as the ripples spread on the surface of a pond; and, anyhow, how much would Jesus rejoice at this harvest of God's glory from thousands of souls making daily one act of thanksgiving more than they otherwise would have done, one Deo gratias, if it were nothing more.

Think of all that is involved of grace, merit, glory, worship, praise, acceptableness in one Deo gratias said with devout intention; and yet with but a little exertion we could send up to the blessed but outraged majesty of God in each year thousands of these supernatural acts!

Why do we let so much that we could do for God slip by without a trial? What a homage of love to Jesus would this easy apostolate of thanksgiving be! Let us begin at once, this very day; for time is flowing from under us, and we have kept God's glory waiting long enough.

Thus also in schools and seminaries, and in domestic families, especially where there are many young children, out of whose pure mouths God has ordained His praise, little associations might be formed to say some quick prayer of thanksgiving daily by themselves and where it seems feasible to make some little act of thanksgiving in common, as well as to endeavor to put more of a thoughtful intention into Grace before and after meals.

The object of these little associations might be to thank God generally for all His goodness to His creatures, or especially for the Incarnation, or again for His mercifully giving us Mary to be our Mother as well as His.

A Catholic school might thus unite morning and afternoon in a little act of thanksgiving for the gift of the most holy Catholic Faith; and thus the children could at once bless God, make reparation for apostasies, and also themselves gain a habit that would be an effectual protection to them in the temptations of later life.

These associations might be connected, if it was thought well, with devotion to the holy angels, whose life is one incessant song of grateful praise, and thus the virtue of purity, the attendant gift of this devotion, might at the same time be fostered in the souls of the youthful members.

If we think aright of the glory of God in one word, if we love Him, these things will not seem small, nor their blessings insignificant. We have much lost time to make up in this matter of thanksgiving.

Oh, what glory cannot one man get for our dearest Lord, if he only lays himself out to do it! St. Jerome,[68] while he lived in the East, often heard the oriental monks intoning their doxology, "Glory be to the Father, and to the Son, and to the Holy Spirit." It took root in him, and he asked Pope Damasus[69] to establish it in the Western Church, where, humanly speaking, but for him it would never have been used.

Who can count the million millions of times that doxology has been used in the West with loving and devout intention? Look how often it comes in the Divine Office.

Now, every time St. Mary Magdalene of Pazzi said it, she accompanied it by a mental offering of herself to the Most Holy Trinity and bowed her head, as it were to the block to be martyred for the Faith.

[68] St. Jerome (c. 347-420).
[69] Pope Damasus (c. 305-384).

Whenever St. Alphonso, in his old age, heard of some good news for the glory of God or the welfare of Holy Church, he cried out with heartfelt emotion, "Gloria Patri, et Filio, et Spiritui Sancto."

Great things are told us of the devotion of the Blessed Paul of the Cross to this doxology, and he taught the same spiritual devotion to his religious.

The lives of the saints would doubtless furnish us with many other devotions of heroic love that have been connected with this doxology.

Yet, if St. Jerome had not one day asked Pope Damasus to introduce it into the Western Church, all this glory would have been lost to God. When men do anything for God, the very least thing, they never know where it will end or what amount of work it will do for Him.

Love's secret, therefore, is to be always doing things for God and not to mind because they are such very little ones. "Cast thy bread upon the running waters; for after a long time thou shalt find it again. In the morning sow thy seed, and in the evening let not thy hand cease, for thou knowest not which may rather spring up, this or that: and, if both together, it shall be the better."[70]

[70] Eccles. 11:1, 6.

Thanksgiving saves souls

Thirdly, this devotion would be of great help in saving many souls. We ourselves by the practice of it should gain such favor with God as would enable us to impetrate graces that are far above the feebleness of our present prayers. We should see such things happen! Such a throwing open of the treasures of God's mercy, such inundations of grace, such obstinate hearts overcome, such new benedictions poured out over the whole Church!

Then, again, by making daily reparation to God for the ingratitude and unmindfulness of sinners, we would appease His anger against them and thus avert from them many judgments and chastisements, both spiritual and temporal.

It is astonishing in how many indirect ways God lovingly allows us to cooperate in the salvation of souls. Would that we were more ingenious in finding them out and more unwearying in the practice of them. Poor souls! We have given you scandals enough; would we could at least equal them now by prayers and by thanksgivings! It does not seem as if the Precious Blood were half our own, till it has become yours also.

May we never forget that there may be souls on earth whose glory God has tied to our zeal and prayer! There may be a dear soul whom God has loved from all eternity and decreed to call it out of nothing in preference to millions of souls He might have created instead; a dear soul whom Jesus thought of by name upon the Cross and offered for it with distinct oblation all His sufferings; a dear soul for whose company Mary yearns in heaven; and whether or not it shall see God, and be His king and priest forever, clothed with incomparable beauty, and crowned with inexpressible gifts, and plunged in an everlasting sea of joy has been hung, by an adorable venture of divine love, upon my unconscious prayer! What an amazing, and also what a ravishing, possibility!

Ah, Lord! When did I see Thee hungry and did not feed Thee; thirsty, and not give Thee a drink? May His answer never cease to sound in my love-frightened ear: "Inasmuch as thou hast not done it unto the least of these my brethren, thou hast not done it unto me."[71]

[71] Cf. Matt. 25:40.

THANKSGIVING WILL
ENRICH ALL AREAS OF
YOUR SPIRITUAL LIFE

But it is time to ask ourselves the important question: what has been our own practice hitherto with regard to the duty of thanksgiving in general? What is our habitual feeling about God's numberless blessings to us? How long a time have we ever spent in summing up God's blessings to us, even when we have been on retreat?

St. Ignatius wisely tells us to commence our examination of conscience every day with counting up the mercies of God and thanking Him for them. Have we so much as kept faithfully to this little practice? Many have regular times in the day for different spiritual duties; have we any time especially set apart for thanksgiving?

Many, again, keep in their prayer books a little note of the things and persons to pray for; have we any similar memento of the blessings for which we desire daily to thank our Heavenly Father? How often have we besieged the throne of grace for weeks and weeks with Our Fathers, Hail Marys, Misereres, Memorares, Rosaries, Communions, and even penances, for something we desired; and when at last our dear Lord condescended to our importunity, what proportion did our thanksgiving bear to our supplication? How long did it last? In what did it consist? With what fervor and increase of love was it accompanied? Was it a single Te Deum, a hurried Deo gratias, and we took with ungraceful eagerness what God held out to us, almost as if it were our wages, and then, beyond a general vague feeling of gratitude, thought nothing more about it ?

Alas! We have all great need to take shame to ourselves in this respect. So far from having an abiding spirit of thanksgiving, or a keen, lifelong recollection of God's mercies, or a loving regularity in the worship and sacrifice of thanksgiving, we go on letting the Holy Spirit Himself touch our hearts with an intimate sense of our obligations to God and our dependence on Him, waiting until He does do so and then feebly responding to His call; so that we let

Him, as it were, ask for our thanks rather than pay them with a free heart and out of an abounding love.

Where we fail is that we do not correspond to His touch; we need His pressure. We would be quick enough to see the wretchedness of all this if a fellow creature did it to us.

But answer these questions honestly to your guardian angels, and then say if you think I exaggerated when I said that the disproportion of thanksgiving to prayer is one of the wonders of the world, and one of its saddest wonders, too.

But what is the cause of all this? I do not care if I write it again and again until you are weary of reading it, if only that would ensure your remembering it. It comes from your perverse refusal to look at God as your Father.

Independent of open sin, there is scarcely a misery that does not come from these hard, dry, churlish views of God. That is the root of the evil. You must lay the axe there, if you really desire to be other than you are. No schemes for self-improvement will stand in the stead of it.

You may meditate, and examine your conscience, and tell your beads, and little enough will come of it, as you have so often found already. How wonderfully people can be regular in making their daily meditation without its ever melting into them! Not a passion is subdued, not an unloveliness smoothed away! They have the custom of prayer without the gift of it. You may do penances, and they will rather harden your heart in a delusion of vainglorious humility than melt into simple, genuine love. The very sacraments will work only like machines out of order.

Whether it is stunted growth in the spiritual life that you deplore, or the absence of all sensible devotion, or incapacity to make and keep generous resolutions, or teasing relapses into unworthy imperfections, or want of reverence in prayer, or lack of sweetness with others, in almost every case the mischief may be traced to an unaffectionate view of God.

You must get clear of this. You must cultivate a filial feeling toward Him. You must pray to the Holy Spirit for His gift of *piety*, whose special office it is to produce this feeling.

Your most prominent idea of God must be as the God "of whom all paternity is named in heaven and on earth."[72] You must remember that the Spirit of Jesus is the one true

[72] Eph. 3:15

Spirit and that He is the Spirit of adoption, whereby we cry, "Abba, Father!"[73]

You will never be right until your view of God as your Father swallows up all your other views of Him, or at least until they are brought into harmonious subordination to that view, which is the sweet soul of the gospel and the life of our Blessed Savior's teaching.

A man could not do better than devote his whole life to be the apostle of this one idea, the compassionate paternity of God.

In matters of spiritual progress, our interests are identical with God's glory. This is another of His loving contrivances. Hence we may still further persuade ourselves to the practice of thanksgiving by reflecting from a spiritual point of view on the benefits to ourselves that result from it.

Growth in holiness is nothing but the continual descent upon us of those fresh graces, which crown every act of correspondence on our part to graces already received; and there is nothing, as we know, that so multiplies graces upon us, or causes God to throw the doors of His treasury so wide open, as the devotion of thanksgiving.

[73] Cf. Rom. 8:15.

But it is not only in this way that it helps us on in holiness. Its effects on our mind must also be taken into account. Many persons try to advance in spirituality and are held back, as it were, by some invisible hand. The fact is, and they do not realize it, they have never been thoroughly converted to God. They have stayed too short a time in the purgative way of the spiritual life, or they have bargained with God and kept back some attachment, or wished to loosen themselves from unworthy habits gently and gradually, so as to be spared the pain of conversion.

Now, thanksgiving swiftly but imperceptibly turns our religion into a service of love; it draws us to take God's views of things, to range ourselves on His side even against ourselves, and to identify ourselves with His interests even when they seem to be in opposition to our own. Hence we are led to break more effectually with the world and not to trail its clouds and mists along with us on our road to heaven.

Hence, also, we come to root and ground ourselves more effectually in the sense of our own vileness and worse than nothingness before God; and what is all this but to make our conversion more thorough and complete?

Neither is the effect of thanksgiving less upon our growth than it is upon our conversion. All growth comes of love; and love is at once both the cause and effect of thanksgiving.

What light and air are to plants, that is the sense of God's presence to the virtues; and thanksgiving makes this sensible presence of God almost a habit in our souls. For it leads us continually to see mercies that we should not otherwise have perceived, and it enables us far more worthily to appreciate their value, and in some degree to sound the abyss of divine condescension out of which they come.

Moreover, the practice of thanksgiving in ourselves leads us to be distressed at the absence of it in others; and this keeps our love of God delicate and sensitive and breeds in us a spirit of reparation, which is especially congenial to the growth of holiness.

Our hearts are enlarged while we are magnifying God; and when our hearts are enlarged, we run the way of His commandments, where we have only walked or crept before. We feel a secret force in overcoming obstacles and in despising fears, and altogether a liberty in well-doing, which we used not to feel before; and all because thanksgiving has made us measure the height of God's goodness and the depth of our vileness; and so nothing looks too much or too hard where the glory of God is concerned. Like Areuna in the time of the pestilence,[74] we give to

[74] 2 Kings 24 (RSV = 2 Samuel 24).

the King as kings ourselves, and in the spirit of kings. Our hearts are crowned with thanksgiving.

It is a great mistake to think lightly of happiness in religion, of enjoyment in religious services, of sweetness in prayer, of gladness in mortification, and of sensible devotion. True it is that when God subtracts them, it is not necessarily in anger or as a chastisement; and whatever be the cause, our plain duty is to submit ourselves to His sweet, though inscrutable, will. But this does not hinder all these things from being mighty aids in the spiritual life, and therefore to be desired and coveted with earnestness, although in a submissive spirit.

Who does not know cases in which everything seems to go wrong because a person has no happiness in religion? Even at Mass and Benediction a veil is over their hearts, which neither music nor brightness, nor yet the divine presence, can penetrate.

God's blessings are as dull to such people as His chastisements are to the generality of men. Prayer is a penance; confession a torture; Communion a very rack. What God blesses for them irritates like a sore. What He fills with peace troubles them with disquietude. They have no light but the gloom of their own perverse moodiness, and they have no song but peevishness. Inquire if such persons have ever had a spirit of thanksgiving, and you will find you have hit exactly on the characteristic omission of their lives.

Perhaps they have been converts to the holy Faith. They have obeyed grace grudgingly. When they were safe in the Church, they would see difficulties everywhere, from the Pope and Roman manners downward. Imaginary evils surrounded every step. There was temporal unhappiness, and was the Faith worth it? There was the annoyance of learning a new religion, and new ceremonies, and this made them snappish. Then preachers said such strong things, and they must complain to a score of people of this, as if everything was to be suited to them.

It was the Assumption, and the dear, good Irish wanted to hear of their Mother's Coronation; but then this important convert was at church and had brought an important Protestant friend with him and should have been consulted, or forewarned. It was so unkind, so injurious, in his presence, to say our Lady had twelve stars on her head. Were they planets or fixed stars? The whole matter is full of difficulties. Really, preachers should be more careful!

Then, in the confessional, it was all so uncomfortable, so coarse, and vulgar, and matter of fact. There was so little smooth talking, and yet much that was so dreadfully to the point.

Thus, from one cause or another, the poor convert has been miserable ever since conversion; and why? Immersed in self, and magnifying self, seeking consolations, and hungering after sympathy, such persons have hardly once fallen like children on their knees to thank God for the miracle of love that brought them where they are.

A thankful heart would have taken joyously all the incipient difficulties of its new position, as a penance for the hard-heartedness that had given grace so much trouble and cost it so many efforts in the process of conversion. But these persons were not thankful, and so they are not happy. Let us thank God that their numbers are so few.

This, however, is another point to be made much of: that happiness in religion comes from the spirit of thanksgiving.

Conclusion

G oing with modern habits of mind to the perusal of the lives of the saints, it seems almost strange to find gratitude — what we might nearly call the old heathen virtue of gratitude — so prominent a characteristic of the saints. It is one of the marks peculiar to all the saints, but more especially to the founders of religious orders and congregations. They seem to exaggerate the little benefits they have received and to make as much of them as if they never could pay them off.

St. Philip had a marvelously long memory for the most trivial kindnesses. St. Ignatius appears sometimes quite absorbed in them, and passes on the obligations as heirlooms to future generations of his order.

The treatment of patrons and founders in the Middle Ages, and the courteous observances of the Church toward them even at solemn times and in sacred places, is a manifestation of the same instinct of sanctity and is, of course, closely connected with the spirit of thanksgiving.

This is not our way now. A change has come over us that betokens something wrong, whatever it may be. Perhaps we do less for each other than we used to. Earlier times and simpler forms of society may, like the beginning of colonies, have excelled in other virtues more than we.

But this much is plain: that we take benefits far too much as matters of course and that we lose with God in consequence. We are so beset with the notion of our own rights, the monomania of our times, that it actually disturbs and perplexes our relations with God, and confuses our theology.

We have so many rights defined and undefined, and we fight so disproportionately for them, that we come to look on almost everything that happens to us as a right or as an attack on our rights. We see this in others, even if we are blind to it in ourselves. We complain again and again that the poor take alms, as if they were rights, not favors. Now, if Catholic theology be true, alms are much closer to being rights, especially to the very poor, than the favors we receive and count as due to us, and as if we were beholden to nothing for them but our own rank and worth.

In these days we canonize self-help as the queen of virtues instead of charity, and this poisons the very fountains of our moral philosophy and distorts our notions of duty.

Then, again, the different classes of society are so coldly divided off one from another, not so much blood from wealth as wealth from mediocrity, and mediocrity from poverty, that it is as if civilization were resolving itself back again into an institution of castes, a state almost worse than promiscuous savagery.

Furthermore, we do good to each other, either through large charitable organizations from which the individual kindness is evaporated and lost, or on so small and niggardly a scale, that there is no scope for a vigorous growth of gratitude.

From whatever cause, gratitude is not a modern virtue, and the absence of it is one of those modern vices against which we must be especially on our guard when we are trying to train our souls on the model of Catholic sanctity.

To some it may appear strange that I should make so much of thanksgiving and treat it as a separate form of devotion to the Blessed Sacrament. But the lack of it is a grievous fault and comes of a most unholy temper.

If a man were shown me who had a long memory for little kindnesses, who never seemed out of debt in his affections, who exaggerated his obligations to others, kept anniversaries of them, and repaid them twenty times over, I would be more struck with the likelihood of his turning out a saint than if I heard that he slept on bare boards, enjoyed the prayer of quiet, had been scourged by devils, and had seen our Blessed Lady.

Appendix

MEDITATIONS FOR
THANKSGIVING
AFTER COMMUNION

C onsidering the difficulty and the importance of making a good thanksgiving after Communion, let me
not seem tedious if I provide my readers with materials for
this purpose: the method of thanksgiving recommended
by Father Lancisius.

I must not be understood to recommend it to anyone
as he gives it. It is far too long and minute and, I believe,
would in most cases smother devotion by the multiplicity
of acts that it involves. The heart must have freer play,
and the whole exercise must be much more simplified. I
give it, therefore, to furnish materials, to serve as a sort
of mine out of which persons with different tastes, or the
same persons at different times, may supply themselves

with food either for reflection or aspiration, as many of the thoughts are both deep and beautiful.

We should draw from it, according as we require, streams of living water to freshen our dry hearts and to adorn them with the variety of devotion. It deserves to be carefully studied, for it really is a treatise of holy living in itself, and that of the most consistent description. It portrays, and would help to form, a definite spiritual character. There are in it wishes taken for granted, and petitions offered to God, at which perhaps we start and tremble. Even these are good for our souls. Lancisius gives them as if no devout soul would dream of shrinking from them.

It is good to be humbled by the thought; and it must humble us to see how far off we are from what we ought to be, and, perhaps, which is more to the point, from what we thought ourselves to be. We are humbled but not discouraged. For if we were discouraged, it would show that we had really no spirituality in us at all and were but standing yet at the starting place, whereas we should by this time have been at least in sight of the blessed goal.

Acts of Humiliation

The acts that Father Lancisius suggested as best to follow immediately after Communion are those of humiliation.

We are to humble ourselves profoundly before God for
the coming of so great a Lord, recalling:

- the sins of our past lives
- our present imperfections and tepidity
- the vileness of our nature compared with the
  divinity of Christ
- our Blessed Lord's perfections as both God and
  man

Acts of Adoration

Then follow acts of adoration:

- Adore the Most Holy Trinity in the Blessed
  Eucharist
- Adore the Sacred Humanity of Jesus existing
  within ourselves at that time
- Adore the same as existing in so many places
  in the Church, wherever the Blessed Sacrament is reserved, rejoicing over His worship
  and honor where the faithful are ever crowd-
  ing to Him, and mourning over His dishonor
  wheresoever He lies without due devotion
  being paid to Him, or where He is perhaps
  actually blasphemed

- Adore with a special adoration the soul of Christ, as filled with all the elements of sanctity, with all merits, and with so ancient, constant, and fruitful a love of us
- Adore the Body of Christ, as having suffered so many and such bitter and unworthy things on our account, and as at length slain for us, and we must imprint spiritual kisses on those parts of His body that for our sakes were the most tormented with wounds and agony

Acts of Thanksgiving

We must give thanks also from the bottom of our hearts for:

- His coming to us in this Communion
- His advent in the Incarnation
- all the merits and examples of virtue during His life, which He left for our good
- the institution of this most Holy Sacrament, and all the other sacraments
- His death and our redemption
- the blessing of creation
- our preservation
- the gift of faith
- our justification

- our perseverance in a state of grace or in a holy calling
- His patience in bearing with our sins and imperfections, and those of others
- the holiness He has granted to so many saints
- the trials and tribulations that we have ever had to undergo
- His assiduous care in leading us along the way of perfection
- all the particular individual blessings we have received from Him
- all the blessings He has conferred on us through others
- all the blessings that God has ever granted, or ever will grant to any creature, especially those that He gave to the sacred humanity of Jesus, to His Blessed Mother, and the rest of the saints and elect

Acts of Oblation

We must offer to God what we have received.
   To the Most Holy Trinity:
- Offer the Blessed Sacrament, which you have received, for all the joy, honor, and

complacency that the Divine Majesty receives therefrom, because of all the blessings it confers on you and others; offer it for your sins and necessities, and those of others, and of your friends and enemies, living or dead.

To our dear Lord, whom you have received, in union with His merits and holy limbs:

- Offer your soul and body with all your faculties, limbs, senses, actions, and repose, desiring only the sanctification of everything about you, that you may be a sort of perpetual holocaust, burning to the delight and honor of the Divine Majesty, consuming yourself and reducing yourself to nothing, purely for God;
- Offer your will to die or to endure anything rather than offend Him again by any deliberate sin, whether mortal or venial.
- Offer your intention always to choose the most perfect things and among them those rather that are most repugnant to your senses, judgment, will, and honor, because you hope thus to gain most glory for God, as well as become more like Jesus crucified.

- Offer your resolution to persevere in the observance of the commandments and counsels of God, and in a perfect life, however full it may be of tribulations.
- Offer your willingness to suffer heavy things that those around you will esteem light, and so you will gain no credit for them.
- Offer your will to seek God alone in all your actions.
- Offer your burning desire to convert all men to His pure love, and your pining for this sweet conversion.

Acts of Petition

From Christ:

- Ask the remission of your sins, both as to the guilt and punishment of them.
- Ask perseverance in His grace and holy living.
- Ask (if you have your spiritual director's leave) for sufferings, sharp, frequent, various, personal, little esteemed or sympathized with by others, hidden, without cause on your part, and without sin either of your own, or of those who afflict you.

- Ask for more of the virtues of humility, poverty, chastity, obedience, faith, hope, charity, prudence, justice, fortitude, temperance, patience, devotion, prayer, discerning of spirits, mortification of the passions, the greatest purity of heart and intention, and all the rest of the virtues.

- Ask for a heart free from all bad actions, unmeritorious or tepid deeds, from all vicious habits, inordinate movements of the passions, and from all debt of temporal punishment, either now or at the hour of death.

- Ask earnestly for grace in all your actions to seek what nature, perfection, and mortification require and to be able to elicit all your actions as intensely as the infused and acquired habits of virtue exist in your interior, so that all your actions may correspond adequately to your knowledge and may most perfectly fulfill in all respects the intentions of the divine government.

- Ask to live a long life in sanctity, and with immense fruit of souls.

- Beg for the grace to treat your body roughly, without thereby injuring greater goods, such as health; and to have some pain sent you at fit times whenever you have any debt of temporal punishment to pay.

+ Beg our Lord to conform your will to His, and, as far as may be, to direct all your faculties, senses, limbs, and actions, as His divinity directed the same things in His sacred humanity.

Petition God the Father:

+ Pray for vigilance and exemplary life in the pastors of His Holy Church, for the conversion of infidels, heretics, schismatics, sinners, and lukewarm souls, and for the perpetual and persevering multiplication of saints, and their advancement in the ways of the Spirit.

+ Pray for the religion and love of justice of rulers, for their mutual concord, their success in lawful undertakings, and their profound submission to the Holy See.

+ Pray for help and consolation for the afflicted in poverty or sickness, for patience for the persecuted and their deliverance, if it be consistent with the greater glory of God.

+ Pray for abundant gifts of grace and glory for your adversaries.

- Pray for the dead—all your adversaries, your relations, friends, and others, especially those for whom few or no prayers are offered—that they may be liberated as soon as possible from purgatory and become your patrons in heaven.
- Pray for those who have asked your prayers, asking God to assist them in the particular respect for which they have desired or needed your prayers.

Acts of Virtue

Acts of adoration

Adore with divine worship that sweet Sacrament received into yourself and reserved in so many churches all through the world. This act of loving adoration may be made more intense by thinking of all those churches in which the Blessed Sacrament is but little honored, or where He is, as it were, a prisoner in the hand of schismatics, or of the countries in which grave sins are committed against His worship.

Acts of faith

- Affirm Christ, whom you have received, to be both true God and true man, and to whose divinity and humanity belong all those things which Holy Church believes of them, or which heretics have denied.

Acts of hope

- Expect from Christ, as God and First Cause, many natural gifts, as well as supernatural graces and glory, and expect the same also through His merits as man.

Acts of charity

- Embrace Him fervently in your interior will as God and man.
- Rejoice that His divinity is so perfect in itself, and in respect of us, that we cannot perfectly know it.
- Exult that His divinity is so worshipped and beloved in heaven by the angels and saints and by just men on earth, and that His body and soul are so unspeakably blessed in heaven, and adorned with such incomparable gifts.
- Grieve deeply that so many sins have been, are being, and will be committed against His dear love by ourselves or by others, and grieve most of all that so many, for whom He has done and

suffered so much, are lost through their own willful perversity; and then, last of all, desire with tenderest love that all sins and imperfections might cease in the world as soon as possible, that the just might be multiplied, and the saints advanced in perfection and perseverance; that infidels and all out of the true Church might be brought to the holy Faith, and that God, and Christ as man, might be honored and loved by men in that way and to that degree in which God desires that He and the sacred humanity of Christ should be loved and honored.

Acts of Contemplation

Contemplate in our dear Lord as God the attributes of His divinity and His other perfections, and elicit different acts with respect to them.

- Consider His self-existence, and ask Him to give us the grace to depend on no one but Him alone, and on superiors only for His sake.
- Reflect on His eternity, and ask Him for long life to serve Him and suffer greatly for Him.
- Look at His omnipresence, and desire that He may be known and loved in all places. We must

make a most burning act of love and adoration to recompense Him for all the sins that are being committed this moment in the boundless temple of His most pure and dread immensity.

- Think of His infinite energy in producing both natural and supernatural effects, and ask Him to give us natural and supernatural gifts of every kind, to the end that we may be as a bait or a net to allure all men and captivate them to His love.

- Consider His infinite wisdom, and ask Him to make us wise in all that regards the instruction of ourselves or others, and to pour out upon us the gifts of counsel, prudence, and discernment of spirits, and growth in virtue, and proficiency in theological studies, without which last we shall do but little for the saving of souls.

- Meditate on His goodness, and pray that in our actions God may see nothing that is not good; but this will be the case only when all our actions are done freely, without imperfections, and for a supernatural end, which is God Himself.

- Think of His eternal generation and person, by which He is constituted Son, and beg of

Him by His divine filiation to grant to us, as far as is possible, liberally and copiously, according to the measure of His ordinary power, all the natural and supernatural perfections of grace and glory that are communicable to His adopted sons, in the same sort as they were communicated to Him then, when He united in Himself the person of the Eternal Word and human nature.

• Ponder His concurrence in the actions of creatures, and implore Him to give us the grace that, as He in each act refers His concurrence in and with us simply to Himself and His own glory as its end, so we in all our actions, without one exception, may work for and because of Him, and may do this so perfectly that there may be nothing in us, direct or indirect, in which God's glory is not sought and found.

Offer Him to the angels and saints: We conclude our thanksgiving by presenting our Blessed Lord, whom we have received in the Holy Eucharist, to all the orders of the beatified spirits:

- To the holy angels we may say, "Behold, you His highest ministers, who do His word, behold the Firstborn of the Eternal Father, whom at that Heavenly Father's bidding you did adore when He entered into the world, and obtain for me the grace to serve Him with the same spirit and truth wherewith you served Him during your probation and serve Him now in your heavenly and blessed life."

- To the patriarchs and prophets we may say, "Behold, you ambassadors of heaven, and partners of the marvelous secrets of God, that Redeemer who was promised from the beginning of the world, whom you desired and so long a time expected, and make me with all the powers and affections of my heart to pant after Him, and to sigh for my Beloved, day and night."

- To the holy Apostles we may say, "Behold, illustrious preachers of the gospel, your beloved Master, whom you did love so ardently with your whole hearts, and make me to love Him fervently above all things, and with my deepest affections."

- To the holy martyrs: "Behold, brave witnesses of the Faith, Christ crucified, for the love of whom you did so willingly shed your blood; oh, gain for me the grace always to be suffering pain for Him, and to live ever on the cross, and that it may be a hard cross, whether nature with her strength fastens me upon it, or the hands of evil men, and then that I may pass straight from the cross unto my Lord."

- To the confessor pontiffs: "Behold, you shepherds of the Lord's flock, the Immaculate Lamb, whom you were once wont to sacrifice to Almighty God in the odor of sweetness on the holy altar, enable me to occupy myself worthily in so great a sacrifice, to offer it aright to God, and, ever associating myself with that sacred Oblation, to offer myself perpetually to Him by good works in the odor of sweetness."

- To confessors religious: "Behold, faithful servants of my Lord, your sweet and beloved Lord, for whom in reality as well as in desire you did forsake all the pleasures of this world; enable me for His love to persevere till death in my state, however dishonorable or poor, and to climb to the height of great holiness for the pure love of God alone."

+ To the holy virgins: "Behold, you spouses of the Immaculate Lamb, Him for whom you did keep your virginity with so much exultation; make me to appear ever before the eyes of your Beloved and mine, pure both in heart and work, and at last, free from all stain of sin and all obligation of punishment, to pass straight from this life to Him in heaven."

+ To all the saints: "Behold, my dearest friends, who are the consolation of my poor soul, the Master, Author, and reward of your sanctity; get me grace to walk as you walked with mighty strides of holiness, so that the increasing series of my years may never find me lingering where I was before, but ever mounting upward to the heights of holiness.

Concluding Father Lancisius's post-Communion meditations

Then say to our dearest Lord:

Now, O my Lord, I retire from Thee for a little while, yet not without Thee! No! For Thou art the consolation, felicity, and every good of my soul.

I commend myself with all vehemence to Thy most ample charity, with all my brothers, friends, and enemies. Love us, O Lord, as much as Thou canst, and inebriate us with Thy love, and transform us into Thy likeness, O joy and exultation of our hearts; and grant that we may live wholly in Thee, be wholly occupied with Thee and for Thee, and that we may have no object in any of our words and actions, within us or without, but only Thee, our Love and our every good; who livest and reignest, forever and ever. Amen.

Last of all say the *Respite:*

Look down, we beseech Thee, O Lord, on this Thy family, for which our Lord Jesus Christ did not hesitate to be delivered into the hands of wicked men, and to suffer the torment of the Cross; who liveth and reigneth with Thee and the Holy Spirit, one God, world without end. Amen.

Biographical Note

FREDERICK WILLIAM FABER

(1814-1853)

Oratorian and devotional writer Frederick William Faber was born in Yorkshire, England, in 1814. The son of an Anglican clergyman, he came under the influence of John Henry Newman, joined Newman's Tractarian Movement, and was ordained in the Anglican church in 1839. He was received into the Catholic Church in 1845, a month after Newman himself became a Catholic, and was ordained a priest in 1847.

In 1846, Fr. Faber established a religious community: the Brothers of the Will of God, or the Wilfridians. Having placed himself in 1848 as a novice under Newman in Newman's new congregation, the Oratory of St. Philip Neri, Faber founded in 1849 an Oratory in London, where, in a tavern turned chapel, he offered nightly services and sermons with hymns and processions of the Blessed Sacrament. He composed three volumes of hymns, including "Faith of Our Fathers." He was noted for his eloquent and moving preaching.

Fr. Faber began his series of forty-nine *Lives of Modern Saints* in 1847. More than mere biographies, these lives demonstrate the development of holiness and the sanctity that can be attained through grace. Fr. Faber is well known for his works on the spiritual life: *All for Jesus*, *Growth in Holiness*, *The Blessed Sacrament*, *The Creator and the Creature*, *The Foot of the Cross*, *Spiritual Conferences*, *The Precious Blood*, and *Bethlehem*. With a focus on the sacraments, prayer, and the Word of God, Fr. Faber's works continue to inspire readers with spiritual insight, moving counsel, and practical ways to grow in holiness.

Sophia Institute

Sophia Institute is a nonprofit institution that seeks to nurture the spiritual, moral, and cultural life of souls and to spread the Gospel of Christ in conformity with the authentic teachings of the Roman Catholic Church.

Sophia Institute Press fulfills this mission by offering translations, reprints, and new publications that afford readers a rich source of the enduring wisdom of mankind.

Sophia Institute also operates two popular online Catholic resources: CrisisMagazine.com and CatholicExchange.com.

Crisis Magazine provides insightful cultural analysis that arms readers with the arguments necessary for navigating the ideological and theological minefields of the day. *Catholic Exchange* provides world news from a Catholic perspective as well as daily devotionals and articles that will help you to grow in holiness and live a life consistent with the teachings of the Church.

In 2013, Sophia Institute launched Sophia Institute for Teachers to renew and rebuild Catholic culture through service to Catholic education. With the goal of nurturing the spiritual, moral, and cultural life of souls, and an abiding respect for the role and work of teachers, we strive to provide materials and programs that are at once enlightening to the mind and ennobling to the heart; faithful and complete, as well as useful and practical.

Sophia Institute gratefully recognizes the Solidarity Association for preserving and encouraging the growth of our apostolate over the course of many years. Without their generous and timely support, this book would not be in your hands.

www.SophiaInstitute.com
www.CatholicExchange.com
www.CrisisMagazine.com
www.SophiaInstituteforTeachers.org

Sophia Institute Press® is a registered trademark of Sophia Institute. Sophia Institute is a tax-exempt institution as defined by the Internal Revenue Code, Section 501(c)(3). Tax I.D. 22-2548708.